This book belongs to:

_____

READ THIS BEFORE YOU START!!

Why is Mental Health So Important?
Mental health is vital to living a healthy, balanced life. It greatly impacts our thoughts, behaviors, and emotions. When we focus on it, virtually every aspect of life can improve. From increasing our productivity to improving our interpersonal relationships, there are so many great benefits to working on out mental health. Sometimes, when dealing with issues such as depression or anxiety, it can be quite difficult to get ourselves out of the constant mind trap of overthinking, negativity, and worrying. Focusing on low stress activities such as coloring is a great way to relax our mind, calm anxiety, reduce stress, and give ourselves a little break. If we pair that with daily positive affirmations, then we have the power to improve our mood and our overall idea of self-worth.

What are Positive Affirmations?
Affirmations are statements that can help you to challenge and overcome self-sabotaging negative thoughts. Affirmations are meant to be powerful and uplifting. When you repeat them out loud, often and you believe in them, you can start to make positive changes. It can be like exercising and how it does our body good, positive affirmations are an exercise for our mind. They can alter our thinking patterns in a positive manner.

Instructions:
Make time in your day to just sit down, take a couple of deep breaths, grab your coloring utensils of choice and repeat each affirmation inside your head as you color every page! Soak up ALL the self-love and positive energy!! Please take the time to discover the calmness and inner peace while you escape the noise, we all have in our head from time to time.

Created by: Kassandra G. Lennox

© 2022 **LENNOX MANAGEMENT LLC**
ALL RIGHTS RESERVED.

This book or any portion thereof may not be reproduced or used in any manner whatsoever without the express written permission of the publisher, except for brief use within a review.

created by @KLENNOX1982 for
@theREALmsKass #kindwordswithKass

TO **GOD** & ABUELA GEORGIE:

for ALWAYS giving me the strength to push through even on the darkest of days. There are no words that can express my deepest gratitude and love for you now and always Abuelita.

TO MY PARENTS
Doug & Sandy:

for raising me to believe that anything was possible with time, effort, pride and dedication.

TO MY SIBLINGS
Kristina & Douglas:

for supporting me in all that I decide to put my heart and soul into.

TO MY SOUL SISTERS
Liane & Jennifer:

for being my sounding board and cheerleaders when others didn't believe in me including myself.

TO MY MENTORS
JILLIAN MURPHY & GRETCHEN HEINEN
AND MY/OUR COMMUNITY:

for motivating me to speak up and out on topics that have always been taboo. Special thanks goes out to all of those who have liked and shared your stories even when it may be difficult or uncharted territory in your life.

Thank you for believing in my safe space created for ALL of us!

created by @KLENNOX1982 for
@theREALmsKass #kindwordswithKass

created by @KLENNOX1982 for
@theREALmsKass #kindwordswithKass

created by @KLENNOX1982 for
@theREALmsKass #kindwordswithKass

created by @KLENNOX1982 for
@theREALmsKass #kindwordswithKass

created by @KLENNOX1982 for
@theREALmsKass #kindwordswithKass

created by @KLENNOX1982 for
@theREALmsKass #kindwordswithKass

created by @KLENNOX1982 for
@theREALmsKass #kindwordswithKass

created by @KLENNOX1982 for
@theREALmsKass #kindwordswithKass

created by @KLENNOX1982 for
@theREALmsKass #kindwordswithKass

created by @KLENNOX1982 for
@theREALmsKass #kindwordswithKass

created by @KLENNOX1982 for
@theREALmsKass #kindwordswithKass

created by @KLENNOX1982 for
@theREALmsKass #kindwordswithKass

created by @KLENNOX1982 for
@theREALmsKass #kindwordswithKass

created by @KLENNOX1982 for
@theREALmsKass #kindwordswithKass

created by @KLENNOX1982 for
@theREALmsKass #kindwordswithKass

created by @KLENNOX1982 for
@theREALmsKass #kindwordswithKass

created by @KLENNOX1982 for
@theREALmsKass #kindwordswithKass

created by @KLENNOX1982 for
@theREALmsKass #kindwordswithKass

created by @KLENNOX1982 for
@theREALmsKass #kindwordswithKass

created by @KLENNOX1982 for
@theREALmsKass #kindwordswithKass

created by @KLENNOX1982 for
@theREALmsKass #kindwordswithKass

created by @KLENNOX1982 for
@theREALmsKass #kindwordswithKass

created by @KLENNOX1982 for
@theREALmsKass #kindwordswithKass

created by @KLENNOX1982 for
@theREALmsKass #kindwordswithKass

created by @KLENNOX1982 for
@theREALmsKass #kindwordswithKass

created by @KLENNOX1982 for
@theREALmsKass #kindwordswithKass

created by @KLENNOX1982 for
@theREALmsKass #kindwordswithKass

created by @KLENNOX1982 for
@theREALmsKass #kindwordswithKass

created by @KLENNOX1982 for
@theREALmsKass #kindwordswithKass

created by @KLENNOX1982 for
@theREALmsKass #kindwordswithKass

created by @KLENNOX1982 for @theREALmsKass #kindwordswithKass

created by @KLENNOX1982 for
@theREALmsKass #kindwordswithKass

created by @KLENNOX1982 for
@theREALmsKass #kindwordswithKass

created by @KLENNOX1982 for
@theREALmsKass #kindwordswithKass

created by @KLENNOX1982 for
@theREALmsKass #kindwordswithKass

created by @KLENNOX1982 for
@theREALmsKass #kindwordswithKass

created by @KLENNOX1982 for
@theREALmsKass #kindwordswithKass

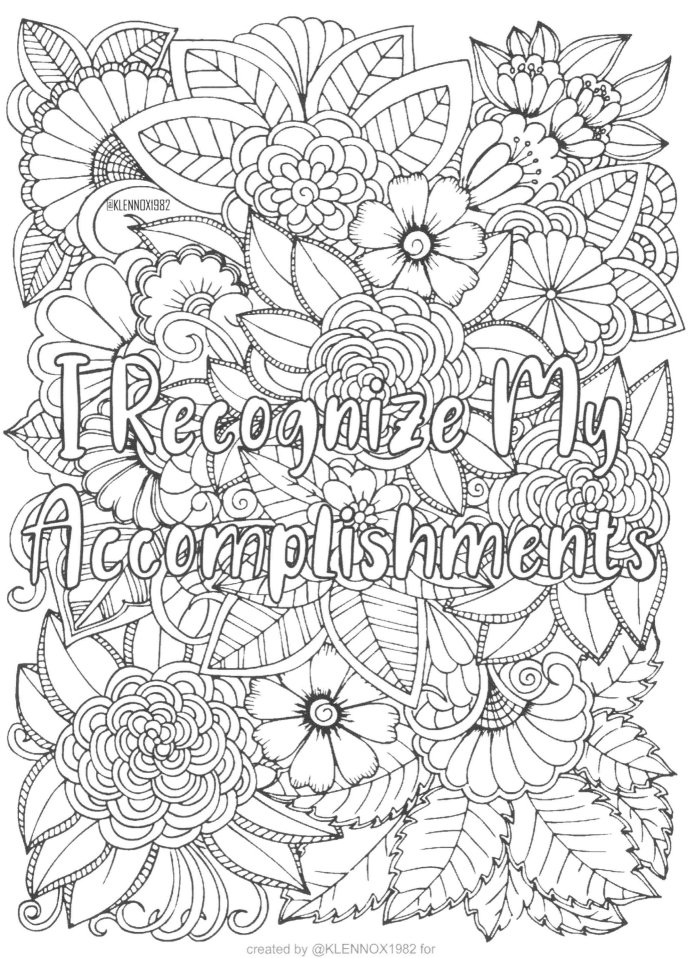

created by @KLENNOX1982 for
@theREALmsKass #kindwordswithKass

created by @KLENNOX1982 for
@theREALmsKass #kindwordswithKass

created by @KLENNOX1982 for @theREALmsKass #kindwordswithKass

created by @KLENNOX1982 for
@theREALmsKass #kindwordswithKass

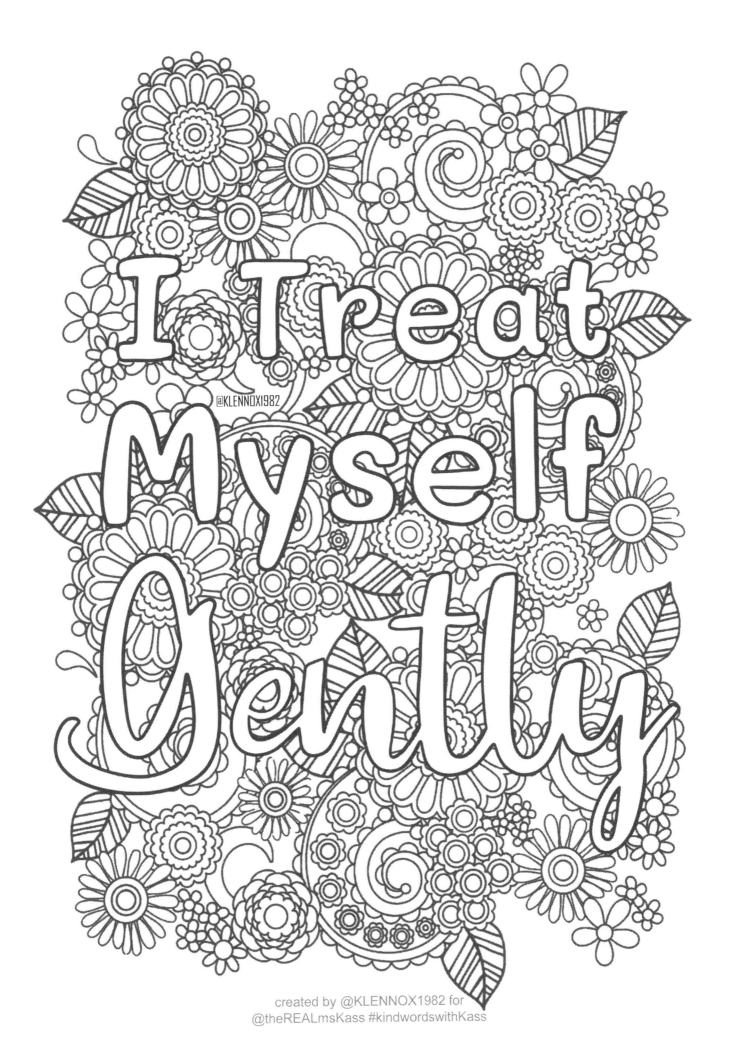

created by @KLENNOX1982 for
@theREALmsKass #kindwordswithKass

created by @KLENNOX1982 for
@theREALmsKass #kindwordswithKass

created by @KLENNOX1982 for
@theREALmsKass #kindwordswithKass

created by @KLENNOX1982 for
@theREALmsKass #kindwordswithKass

created by @KLENNOX1982 for
@theREALmsKass #kindwordswithKass

created by @KLENNOX1982 for
@theREALmsKass #kindwordswithKass

created by @KLENNOX1982 for
@theREALmsKass #kindwordswithKass

created by @KLENNOX1982 for @theREALmsKass #kindwordswithKass

created by @KLENNOX1982 for
@theREALmsKass #kindwordswithKass

created by @KLENNOX1982 for
@theREALmsKass #kindwordswithKass

created by @KLENNOX1982 for
@theREALmsKass #kindwordswithKass

created by @KLENNOX1982 for
@theREALmsKass #kindwordswithKass

created by @KLENNOX1982 for
@theREALmsKass #kindwordswithKass

created by @KLENNOX1982 for
@theREALmsKass #kindwordswithKass

@KLENNOX1982

Made in the USA
Columbia, SC
01 December 2023